Rosé
COCKTAILS

Rosé
COCKTAILS

40 deliciously different
pink-wine based drinks

Julia Charles
photography by Alex Luck

RYLAND PETERS & SMALL
LONDON • NEW YORK

Text copyright © Julia Charles 2018
Design and photographs copyright ©
Ryland Peters & Small 2018

Dedication

For my Bestest, Alison – Patsy to my
Edina and ALWAYS there whenever
I need a top up.

Senior Designer Barbara Zuñiga
Editor Nathan Joyce
Head of Production Patricia Harrington
Editorial Director Julia Charles
Art Director Leslie Harrington
Publisher Cindy Richards
Drinks Stylist Tara Garnell
Prop Stylist Luis Peral
Indexer Hilary Bird

First published in 2018 by
Ryland Peters & Small
20–21 Jockey's Fields
London WC1R 4BW
and
341 E 116th Street
New York, 10029
www.rylandpeters.com

10 9 8 7 6 5 4 3 2 1

ISBN: 978-1-84975-969-4

A CIP record for this book is available
from the British Library. US Library of
Congress CIP data has been applied for.
Printed in China

Acknowledgements
Big thanks to all the willing guinea pigs
who gamely sipped my creations and to
my generous and charming bar owner
friends: Michael Browne, Natasha and
Markus Lang; Theo and Zuzana Roussos;
and Nikos Antiparian. Also to Leslie, Alex,
Luis and Tara for such beautiful images.

Contents

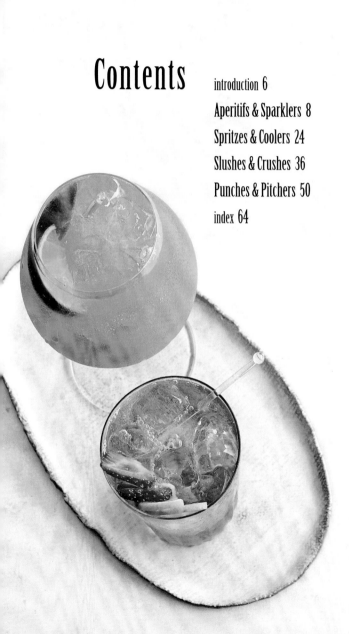

Introduction

It's easy to think of rosé wine as a summertime-only treat. During the warmer months, frosted bottles of 'the pink stuff' can be seen nestling in ice buckets on al fresco restaurant tables the world over. But rosé's growing popularity proves it doesn't have to be just a summer fling. In all its varied styles, from dry to sweet, light to fruity and elegant to spicy, it is a deliciously drinkable choice all year round and makes a surprisingly versatile cocktail ingredient too.

Simply put, rosé wine is made when the juice of red wine is strained from its skins before it becomes too dark. The grape variety and method used to make the wine therefore dictate the intensity of its finished colour and flavour. When creating these recipes, it made sense for me to first taste-test a good cross-section of rosés and take my lead from there – sometimes the bouquet alone was a strong enough hint! I found that some have a sharp, tangy strawberry freshness, others a juicer watermelon mouth-feel, many a bright, cherry ripeness or a pomegranate zing. Some have distinctly floral notes such as rose or hibiscus, or a pleasing herbaceous earthiness. Once I had identified the range of flavour notes already present in a rosé, instinctively adding fresh juices, spirits, liqueurs and syrups that complement these made perfect sense, and helped me on my way to create some conversation-starting cocktails. I've recommended a style of wine within each recipe, but the basic rule is: a dark, medium or sweet rosé works best in strongly-flavoured cocktails and especially frozen drinks, as the colour diminishes after freezing and a pale, dry or off-dry rosé works best in more subtle drinks, such as floral cocktails.

When buying wine for your cocktails it's not important to go for the most expensive bottles. A lot of delicious and very good value rosés are now available. If the recipe requires sweet, fruity rosé, a Californian Zinfandel (or 'blush') is the wine to go for. It is the wine that has lead the 'drink pink' craze and accounts for 85% of rosé sales in the US. It's often a vivid bubble-gum pink with candyfloss/cotton candy, watermelon, raspberry and strawberry flavours. If you need a dry, elegant rosé, choose one from the Provence region of France. They are very pale pink, and though they vary in style tend to be dry, fresh and

crisp with green apple and floral notes. Spain and Portugal's ruby-red rosés can also be dry and off-dry, but are usually bolder and fruity with undertones of red berries, orange, hibiscus and a touch of allspice, making them perfect for spritzes and punches. Vivid deep pink Italian rosé made with Montepulciano grapes is a pleasing, juicy all-rounder. I also found some good value bottles from Chile and Romania (both Cabernet Sauvignon blends), which had a deep colour with red wine-flavours of cherry jam/jelly, blackberry and peppery spice. When it comes to pink fizz, styles vary greatly from dry to sweet. A rosé Prosecco or Asti from Italy are generally safe choices, though Asti is slightly lower in alcohol and a little sweeter. Cava from Spain is rich and biscuity, while a Crémant from France can have pleasing frothy bubbles. Of course, go for a pink Champagne if you want a decadent cocktail for a special occasion. A good rule of thumb with fizz is that a dry one with strong bubbles works well with syrups and fruit liqueurs, and a sweeter less bubbly one is best with spirits and in punches. Above all, buy what you like to drink on its own and what works within your budget, and you will find a cocktail here to suit it.

To create these mouth-watering cocktails, you will need a cocktail shaker, a 'muddler', a small range of glassware and plenty of ice trays. An ice-crushing machine is useful, and for the frosés and slushes a blender and some 1 litre/ quart freezer-proof sealable containers. Many of the recipes in this book call for a well-chilled bottle of rosé, but if you forgot to put it in the fridge don't panic! Simply wrap it in a wet kitchen cloth and pop it in the freezer for 10 minutes.

Aperitifs & Sparklers

Blackberry Bellini

A classic Venetian bellini is white peach purée paired with Prosecco but the sour-sweetness of ripe blackberries works beautifully here with pink fizz.

4 fresh blackberries, plus 1 extra, to garnish

1 teaspoon white caster/granulated sugar

4 ice cubes

30 ml/1 oz. vodka

2 teaspoons freshly squeezed lemon juice

well-chilled rosé Prosecco, to top up

serves 1

Put the 4 blackberries and sugar in a cocktail shaker and gently muddle with a muddler or handle of a rolling pin.

Add the ice cubes, vodka and lemon juice to the shaker and shake until cold, about 20 seconds. Strain into a Champagne flute, top up with cold rosé Prosecco and garnish with a blackberry on a cocktail stick. Serve at once.

Kir Blush

A kir (chilled white wine with a dash of cassis) is a staple of the Parisian café scene.
This simple variation pairs a fruity rosé with softer raspberry crème de framboise.

30 ml/1 oz. crème de framboise

**about 125 ml/½ cup dry but fruity rosé, well chilled
(a French rosé from the Rhône or Bordeaux works well here)**

serves 1

Pour the crème de framboise into the base of a white wine glass,
then top up with cold rosé. Serve at once.

Chambles

The decadent black raspberry liqueur Chambord adds extra fruitiness
with just a hint of creamy vanilla to a glass of sparkling rosé.

30 ml/1 oz. Chambord

**about 125 ml/½ cup sparkling rosé, well chilled
(a dry rosé Crémant or pink Champagne both work well here)**

a fresh raspberry, to garnish

serves 1

Pour the Chambord into the base of a tall flute, then top up with
cold sparkling rosé. Garnish with a fresh raspberry. Serve at once.

Pom Pom

Traditionally used in a Harvey Wallbanger, here Galliano's vanilla-anise
and herby notes really enhance the pomegranate.

10 ml/¼ oz. Galliano

40 ml/1½ oz. 100% pomegranate juice, well chilled

dry sparkling rosé, well chilled, to top up (a pink Crémant works well here)

a few pomegranate seeds and a sprig of fresh mint, to garnish

serves 1

Pour the Galliano and pomegranate juice into a flute and top up with cold sparkling rosé.
Garnish with a few pomegranate seeds and a sprig of mint. Serve at once.

Hibiscus Fizz

Hibiscus flowers have a delicious raspberry and rhubarb flavour that pairs beautifully
with the berry fruit notes of rosé. I've also added a splash of white vermouth to balance
the sweetness and bring a little more depth to the drink.

1 wild hibiscus flower from a jar of flowers in syrup

2–3 teaspoons Monin hibiscus syrup
(or use the syrup from the jar of hibiscus flowers if there is enough)

40 ml/1½ oz. Lillet white vermouth

sparkling rosé, well chilled, to top up (a Cava Rosado works well here)

serves 1

Put a hibiscus flower in the bottom of a wide-necked Champagne coupe or martini glass
(with the petals reaching upwards). Gently pour in the hibiscus syrup and Lillet and top up
with cold sparkling rosé. Serve at once.

Cranberry & Orange Sparkler

This is the ideal companion to a celebratory breakfast or brunch. It's light, refreshing and if you use an Italian Vino Frizzante, it will be a little lower in alcohol than a Prosecco or Champagne-based cocktail, so perfect for drinking before midday!

10 ml/¼ oz. Cointreau or other orange-flavoured liqueur

40 ml/1½ oz. cranberry juice, well chilled

80–100 ml/2½–3⅓ oz. lightly sparkling rosé, well chilled
(an Italian Rosato Vino Frizzante works well)

orange zest and/or fresh cranberries, to garnish

serves 1

Pour the Cointreau and cranberry juice into a Champagne flute and top up with cold sparkling rosé. Garnish with a twist of orange zest and/or a few fresh cranberries on a cocktail stick. Serve at once.

Pimm's in the Pink

This deliciously sweet and fruity cocktail tastes like a strawberry bon bon in a glass, but don't be lulled into a false sense of security as it packs quite a punch!

2–3 strawberries, hulled and finely sliced

20 ml/¾ oz. strawberry syrup
(see page 37) or grenadine

40 ml/1½ oz. London dry gin

50 ml/1¾ oz. sweet, fruity rosé,
(a Californian Zinfandel works well here)

15 ml/½ oz. Pimm's No 1. Cup

15 ml/½ oz. freshly squeezed lemon juice

a strawberry, to garnish

ice cubes

serves 1–2

Combine all the ingredients in a cocktail shaker filled halfway with ice cubes and shake until well chilled, about 20 seconds. Strain into a martini glass, garnish with a strawberry and serve at once.

Rosy Glow

Here is a rather special sipper for lovers of bourbon. Tangy with warming, smoky undertones, try this as an alternative to a hot toddy on a cold day. As its name suggests, it brings a flush to even the palest of cheeks...

100 ml/3⅓ oz. sweet rosé, well chilled (a Californian Zinfandel works well here)

40 ml/1½ oz. bourbon or whiskey

30 ml/1 oz. smooth fresh orange juice

an orange wheel, to garnish

ice cubes

serves 1

Shake all of the ingredients in a cocktail shaker half-filled with ice until cold, about 20 seconds. Strain into an ice-filled old-fashioned glass and garnish with the orange wheel. Serve at once.

Rosé Garden

This sophisticated cocktail has a moreish sharp and sweet, almost sherbety taste that keeps you hooked until the very last sip.

2 large fresh basil leaves, washed and patted dry

60 ml/2 oz. rosé, well chilled
(a pale, dry Provençal-style is good here)

30 ml/1 oz. St-Germain elderflower liqueur

40 ml/1½ oz. freshly squeezed lemon juice

1½ teaspoons Strawberry Syrup (see page 37)

a fresh basil leaf and/or elderflowers, to garnish

ice cubes

serves 1

Muddle the basil leaves in a cocktail shaker with a muddler or the end of a rolling pin. Add 4–5 ice cubes followed by the wine, St-Germain elderflower liqueur, lemon juice and strawberry syrup.

Shake until chilled then, strain into a small cocktail coupette or wine glass. Garnish with a basil leaf and/or elderflowers and serve at once.

Petal

This is an elegant drink, both in appearance and flavour, with a delicate,
rose-scented perfume that's reminiscent of Turkish delight.

1 large fresh strawberry, hulled

25 ml/¾ oz. sugar syrup

10 ml/¼ oz. freshly squeezed lime juice

10 ml/¼ oz. rosewater

100 ml/3 oz. sparkling rosé, well chilled
(a rosé Crémant or pink Champagne work well)

edible rose petal, to garnish
ice cubes

serves 1

In a shaker, lightly muddle the strawberry and sugar syrup. Once pulped, add the lime
juice and rosewater and shake for a few seconds. Strain into an ice-filled old-fashioned
glass and top up with sparkling rosé. Garnish with a rose petal and serve at once.

Lavender Rosé Royale

A strong candidate for my new favourite aperitif, this gin-based delight is similar
to a French 75 in style with the lavender giving it a subtle floral note.

2 large strawberries, hulled

60 ml/2 oz. floral gin (I like to use Bloom)

15 ml/½ oz. freshly squeezed lemon juice

15 ml/½ oz. Monin lavender syrup

200 ml/¾–1 cup extra-dry sparkling
rosé, well chilled (a rosé Vino Spumante
works well)

edible flowers, to garnish
ice cubes

serves 2

Put the strawberries into a cocktail shaker and muddle with a muddler or the end of
a wooden rolling pin. Once pulped, add the gin, lemon juice, lavender syrup and 4–5 ice
cubes. Shake until chilled, about 20 seconds. Strain the mixture into Champagne coupes,
top up with the sparkling rosé and garnish with edible flowers. Serve at once.

Pink Gimlet

A classic drink is often one whose beauty lies in its simplicity.
This twist on a gimlet, the crisp and reviving aperitif, is a shameless treat
for the ever-growing number of gin devotees out there.

75 ml/2½ oz. very pale dry rosé, well chilled
(a pale, dry Provençal-style works well here)
25 ml/¾ oz. London dry gin (I like to use Tanqueray)
25 ml/¾ oz. Rose's lime cordial
a lime zest, to flavour and garnish
ice cubes
serves 1

Pour the wine, gin and lime cordial into an ice-filled cocktail shaker, stir with
a bar spoon until very cold then strain into a martini glass.

Twist the lime zest to release its citrus oil on top of the drink. Garnish the rim
of the glass with the zest or simply float it on the surface of the drink. Serve at once.

Spritzes & Coolers

Spanish Fruit Cup

Here is a fresh take on a classic red-wine sangria. Fruity and citrusy, this is a deliciously thirst-quenching punch to serve at a summer party or beach barbecue.

100 ml/3⅓ oz. fruity rosé, well chilled (a Spanish Garnacha works well here)

50 ml/1¾ oz. smooth fresh orange juice

10 ml/¼ oz. Spanish brandy

10 ml/¼ oz. Cointreau (or other orange-flavoured liqueur)

200 ml/¾–1 cup Fever-Tree Mediterranean tonic water
(or any unflavoured tonic water if Fever-Tree not available)

orange and lemon wheels and green apple slices

a fresh strawberry, to garnish

ice cubes

serves 1

Pour all of the ingredients, the tonic last, into a large ice-filled balloon/copa glass and stir gently with a bar spoon. Add a selection of the fruit slices. Garnish the rim of the glass with a strawberry slice. Serve at once.

NOTE: This also makes a wonderful pitcher drink, so simply use a 750-ml/25-oz. bottle of rosé and multiply the other ingredients by 7 to serve 6–8 people.

Rosé Aperol Spritz

Bitter-sweet Aperol has seen a massive rise in popularity since its signature serve, the Aperol spritz took the international bar scene by storm. This recipe peps it up further with the addition of sparkling rosé Prosecco, fragrant passion fruit juice and a hint of zesty lime.

50 ml/1¾ oz. Aperol

25 ml/¾ oz. passion fruit juice (I like to use Rubicon)

1 teaspoon freshly squeezed lime juice

75 ml/2½ oz. rosé Prosecco, well chilled

lime wedges, to serve

ice cubes

serves 1

Fill a large balloon/copa glass with ice cubes. Pour in the Aperol, passion fruit juice and lime juice. Stir with a bar spoon and top up with the cold rosé Prosecco. Garnish with a couple of wedges of lime and serve at once with a straw.

Strawberry Rosé Spritzer

A gentler version of the classic Aperol spritz that is deliciously light, fresh and fruity with an enticing strawberry scent. Serve as a summer aperitif.

15 ml/½ oz. Strawberry Syrup (see page 37)

50 ml/1¾ oz. Aperol

75 ml/2½ oz. fruity rosé wine, well chilled (a Chilean Cabernet-based blend works well here)

15 ml/½ oz. freshly squeezed lemon juice

about 200 ml/¾–1 cup soda water

strawberries and lemon slices, to garnish

ice cubes

serves 1

Pour the strawberry syrup into a highball glass or balloon/copa glass. Add the Aperol, rosé and lemon juice and stir. Add plenty or ice cubes and top with up with soda water to taste, but no more than 200 ml/¾–1 cup. Garnish with sliced strawberries and lemon slices. Serve at once.

Watermelon Rosé Margarita

This lip-smackingly good margarita will thrill existing fans of the classic
who are looking for something completely new.

about 500 g/1 lb. fresh watermelon flesh,
deseeded and cubed

lime wedge and salt, to rim the glass

60 ml/2 oz. silver tequila

45 ml/1½ oz. triple sec

30 ml/1 oz. freshly squeezed lime juice

60 ml/2 oz. Watermelon & Rosé Syrup
(see below)

60 ml/2 oz. watermelon juice
(from flesh, see method)

60 ml/2 oz. sweet, fruity rosé, well chilled
(a Californian Zinfandel works well here)

lime wedges and watermelon slices,
to garnish

ice cubes

Serves 2–4

To make your own watermelon juice (which you will need for both the syrup
and the cocktail), put the watermelon cubes in a blender and blend until puréed.
Strain the liquid through a fine-mesh sieve/strainer into a jug/pitcher. Discard the fruit
pulp and any seeds, and reserve the watermelon juice.

Place the salt on a plate. Rim the glass with a lime wedge, then dip the glass into the
salt to coat. Discard the lime wedge. Pop the glass in the freezer to chill until needed.

Fill a cocktail shaker with ice cubes. Add the tequila, triple sec, lime juice, watermelon
and rosé syrup, watermelon juice and rosé. Shake until cold, about 20 seconds. Pour the
mixture into margarita glasses. Garnish with a lime wedge and a slice of watermelon.
Serve at once.

Watermelon & Rosé Syrup

125 ml/½ cup sweet, fruity rosé wine (a Californian Zinfandel works well here)
125 ml/½ cup fresh watermelon juice (see method above)
250 g/1¼ cups white sugar

Combine the rosé, watermelon juice and sugar in a saucepan over a medium heat. Bring
to the boil while whisking constantly until the sugar dissolves. Turn off the heat and let
the mixture cool to room temperature. Strain into a clean screw-top jar. You can store
the syrup in the fridge for up to 3 weeks.

Rojito

The mint gives this pimped-up mojito an unbeatable tongue-tingling freshness.

3 fresh mint sprigs, rinsed and patted dry, plus an extra sprig to garnish

2 teaspoons light brown sugar

about 1 tablespoon pink peppercorns

175 ml/¾ cup dry rosé, well chilled (a Chilean Cabernet-based blend works well here)

chilled soda water, to top up

ice cubes

serves 1

Add the mint sprigs to a cocktail shaker with the sugar and 5 pink peppercorns. Muddle until the mint is crushed and the liquid has been extracted. Strain into a tumbler and pour in the wine. Stir and add ice cubes. Top up with soda water then garnish with a mint sprig and a few crushed pink peppercorns. Serve at once with a straw.

Rum 'n' Rosé on the Rocks

This laid-back drink has a distinct feel of the Deep South, worthy of sipping on any porch swing.

30 ml/1 oz. dark rum (I like to use Flor de Caña 7 year old)

15 ml/½ oz. rosé vermouth (a dark syrupy one is best)

75 ml/2½ oz. bottled French peach juice or purée (see note on page 51)

50 ml/1¾ oz. fruity rosé, well-chilled (a Chilean Cabernet/Shiraz works well here)

1–2 teaspoons raw cane sugar syrup, to taste (optional)

chilled soda water, to top up

a slice of fresh peach and a fresh mint sprig, to garnish

ice cubes

serves 1

Put a rocks glass in the freezer for 5 minutes to frost. Remove it from the freezer and fill with ice cubes. Add the rum, rosé vermouth, peach juice and cold rosé to the glass. Stir to mix and then add 1–2 teaspoons of sugar syrup to taste. Garnish with a slice of fresh peach and a fresh mint sprig. Serve at once.

Cucumber Cooler

This simple and elegant recipe combines a homemade cucumber-infused syrup with ice-cold rosé to create a drink as welcome as a fresh breeze on a warm evening.

15 ml/½ oz. Cucumber Syrup (see below)

**about 175 ml/¾ cup sparkling rosé, well chilled
(a dry yet fruity Cava Rosado works well here)**

a long sliver of cucumber

serves 1

Add the cucumber syrup to the glass and top up with cold sparkling rosé.
Garnish with a long single sliver of cucumber and serve at once.

Cucumber Syrup

Put 250 ml/1 cup of water in a small saucepan with 225 g/1 cup white granulated sugar.
Bring to the boil and let simmer for a minute until clear and slightly thickened. Take off
the heat and add the chopped flesh and skin of about half a medium cucumber. Leave
to cool and transfer to a clean screw-top jar. Refrigerate (for a few hours or overnight
if possible) to marinate, then strain the syrup, discard the cucumber pieces, and return
the syrup to the jar. The syrup will keep in the fridge for up to 3 weeks.

B&B

Strawberries and basil are one of nature's little flavour-pairing miracles, so bringing them together in a glass of rosé fizz that's already bursting with berry notes is a treat.

a mix of small strawberries (hulled), blackberries, raspberries and blueberries

15 ml/½ oz. Basil Syrup (see below)

10 ml/¼ oz. freshly squeezed lemon juice

200 ml/¾–1 cup sparkling rosé (a Cava Rosado works well here)

basil leaves and berries, to garnish

serves 1

First pop a berry into each compartment of an ice cube tray. Top up with filtered water and put in the freezer until frozen solid. Pour the basil syrup into a large wine glass. Add the lemon juice and top up with the cava. Add 4–5 berry-filled ice cubes to the glass. Garnish with a basil sprig and a few fresh berries and serve at once.

Basil Syrup

Combine 250 ml/1 cup water, 225 g/1 cup white sugar and a large handful of fresh basil leaves in a small saucepan. Bring to the boil, then remove from the heat and let sit for about 30 minutes. Strain into a screw-top jar and discard the leaves. Refrigerate but note that this syrup loses its colour and turns brown so is best used within 2 days.

Blooming Lovely

I first tasted orange blossom extract in pastiera, an Easter cake served in Naples. It has an indefinable flavour that isn't exactly floral, so it adds intrigue to this elegant spritzer.

4 dashes Peychaud's bitters

15 ml/½ oz. St-Germain elderflower liqueur

¼ teaspoon orange blossom extract

½ teaspoon sugar syrup

120 ml/4 oz. dry sparkling rosé, well chilled

(a pink Champagne works well here)

2 lemon zests

edible flowers, to garnish

ice cubes

serves 1

Pour the bitters, elderflower liqueur, orange blossom extract and sugar syrup into a white wine glass and add a few ice cubes. Top up with Champagne, squeeze the lemon zests over the drink and discard. Stir, garnish with an edible flower and serve at once.

Slushes & Crushes

Classic Strawberry Frosé

Nothing beats a frosted glass of wine on a summer's day, except an ice-blended frosé! Taking just a little time to make the strawberry syrup pays off as your rosé will lose some oomph during freezing so this addition boosts both the fruity flavour and pink hue of the drink.

1 x 750-ml/25-oz. bottle full-flavoured, full-bodied, dark-coloured rosé
(a Pinot Noir or Merlot works well here)
100 ml/3⅓ oz. Strawberry Syrup (see below)
45 ml/1½ oz. freshly squeezed lemon juice
crushed ice
finely pared lemon zest, to garnish
serves 3–4

Pour the rosé into a freezerproof container and transfer to the freezer. Leave until almost frozen, about 4–5 hours. Remove from the freezer and scrape the frozen rosé into the cup of a blender. Add the strawberry syrup, lemon juice and a large scoop of crushed ice. Blend until smooth. Pour the mixture back into the freezerproof container and return to the freezer for about 35–40 minutes, just until the mixture is thickened but you can easily break up the crystals with a fork. Spoon into glasses, garnish with the lemon zest and serve at once with straws.

Strawberry Syrup

Put 250 ml/1 cup of water in a small saucepan with 225 g/1 cup white sugar. Bring to the boil and let simmer until clear and slightly thickened. Take off the heat and add the chopped flesh of half a 250-g/9-oz. punnet of strawberries. Leave to cool, strain, discard the strawberries and transfer the syrup to a clean screw-top jar. It will keep in the fridge for up to 3 weeks.

Rosé, Watermelon, Lime & Mint Frosé

Here's how to survive the next heatwave. Get some booze in the blender and serve up this tooth-tingling and absurdly refreshing adults-only frozen treat.

1 x 750-ml/25-oz. bottle full-flavoured, full-bodied, dark-coloured rosé
(a Pinot Noir or Merlot works well here)

250 ml/1 cup fresh watermelon juice (see page 29)

60 ml/2 oz. Watermelon & Rosé Syrup (see page 29)

45 ml/1½ oz. freshly squeezed lime juice

30 ml/1 oz. vodka

5–6 fresh mint leaves, rinsed and patted dry

lime wheel, watermelon balls and finely pared lime zest, to garnish

serves 3–4

Pour the rosé and watermelon juice into a freezerproof container. Stir to mix, then freeze until solid. Remove from the freezer and allow it to defrost for about 35–40 minutes, until you can break it up with a fork but it's still holding plenty of ice crystals.

Scoop into the cup of a blender and add the rosé and watermelon syrup, lime juice, vodka and mint leaves. Blend for about 30 seconds until pale pink and foamy and speckled with green mint. Pour into serving glasses, add a lime wheel and balls of watermelon on a stick and lime zest to garnish. Serve at once with straws.

Twisted Pineapple Frosé

If a Hawaiian luau is your idea of the ultimate summer party, then here is a tropical take on a frosé, perfect for the next time you plan to have some serious fun in the sun.

1 x 750-ml/25-oz. bottle full-flavoured, full-bodied, dark-coloured rosé
(a Pinot Noir or Merlot works well here)

250 ml/1 cup fresh pineapple juice

45 ml/1½ oz. Bacardi or other white rum

30 ml/1 oz. sugar syrup

30 ml/1 oz. freshly squeezed lime juice

½ a fresh red chilli/chile, deseeded and finely chopped, plus extra to garnish (optional)

pineapple leaf and/or pineapple wedge, to garnish

serves 3–4

Pour the rosé and pineapple juice into a freezerproof container. Stir to mix and freeze until solid. Remove from the freezer and allow it to defrost for about 35–40 minutes, until you can break it up with a fork but it's still holding plenty of ice crystals.

Scoop into the cup of a blender and add the Bacardi, sugar syrup, lime juice and chilli/chile. Blend for about 30 seconds until foamy and speckled with red chilli/chile. Spoon into serving glasses, add a pineapple leaf and/or a pineapple wedge and a sprinkling of red chilli/chile to garnish (optional). Serve immediately with straws.

Sparkling Raspberry & Rosé Caipirinha

For me a caipirinha is THE summer drink and I'd take it over the more popular mojito every time. The eye-watering sharpness of the limes is strangely thrilling and the pleasure for me lies in trying to drain every last sugary sip from the glass as the ice melts.

8 juicy raspberries, plus 1 extra to garnish

1½–2 teaspoons raw cane sugar

½ a lime, cut into 4 wedges

30 ml/1 oz. cachaça (Brazilian sugar-cane spirit)

60–90 ml/2–3 oz. well-chilled sparkling rosé Prosecco

crushed ice

serves 1

Combine the raspberries, sugar and lime in a rocks glass and muddle the raspberries with a muddler or end of a wooden rolling pin until smashed. Fill with crushed ice, pour over the cachaça and stir. Top up with more crushed ice and stir once using a straw. Garnish with a raspberry and serve at once with straws.

The Black Rosé

A refreshing twist on a caipiroska, this is a pleasing mix of tart and fruity, thanks to the combination of a dry rosé floated over muddled blackberries with a cheeky splash of vodka.

3–4 juicy blackberries, plus 1 extra to garnish

1 teaspoon raw cane sugar

freshly squeezed juice of 1 lime

20 ml/¾ oz. vodka

100 ml/3⅓ oz. pale, dry rosé (a French Grenache-based blend works well here)

lime wheel, to garnish

crushed ice

serves 1

Put the blackberries and sugar in a rocks glass and muddle with a muddler or end of a wooden rolling pin until the berries are crushed. Add the lime juice. Tip in a few scoops of crushed ice, then pour over the vodka and wine. Stir once and top up with another scoop of crushed ice. Garnish with a blackberry and lime wheel. Serve at once with straws.

West Coast Sunset

Not so much a cocktail as theatre – this is all about the fun of recreating the visual spectacle of a beautiful pink and orange evening sky in a glass.

1 x 500-ml/1-pint tub mango sorbet (you will need 1 large scoop per serving)
2 teaspoons grenadine
well-chilled sparkling rosé, to top up (a fruity Italian Rosato Frizzante works well here)
a squeeze of fresh lime or orange juice, as preferred
serves 1

Remove the mango sorbet from the freezer 10 minutes before assembling the cocktail to allow it to soften. Pour the grenadine into a large martini glass or margarita coupe. Using an ice cream scoop, add a nice round ball of mango sorbet to the glass. Pour over the sparkling rosé to top up just before serving and add a squeeze of fresh lime or orange juice just to season. Serve at once with both a small spoon and a straw.

Scroppinko

This is my variation on the classic Italian sgroppino, which is a delicious blend of lemon sorbet, Prosecco and vodka. Serve in place of dessert for a zesty end to a rich meal.

1 x 500-ml/1-pint tub lemon sorbet (you will need about 3 small balls per serving)
1 juicy raspberry
30 ml/1 oz. raspberry-flavoured vodka
well-chilled sparkling rosé, to top up (a fruity Italian Rosato Frizzante works well here)
finely pared lemon zest, to garnish
serves 1

Remove the lemon sorbet from the freezer 10 minutes before assembling the cocktail to allow it to soften. Drop the raspberry into a narrow glass and add the raspberry vodka. Using a melon baller, add 3–4 small balls of lemon sorbet to the glass. Top up with Prosecco, garnish with lemon zest and serve at once with a straw.

Rosa-rita

A delicious twist on a margarita with an unexpected hint of spicy heat.

2 large chunks of fresh watermelon flesh
1 small slice of fresh red chilli/chile, deseeded
35 ml/1¼ oz. gold tequila
15 ml/½ oz. Rosemary Syrup (see below)
20 ml/¾ oz. pink grapefruit juice
1 teaspoon freshly squeezed lime juice

a splash of very sweet, fruity rosé
(a Californian Zinfandel works well here)
crushed ice
watermelon wedge, slice of red chilli/chile
and fresh rosemary sprig, to garnish

serves 1

Put the watermelon and chilli/chile in a cocktail shaker and crush with a muddler or end of a wooden rolling pin. Add the tequila, rosemary syrup, grapefruit and lime juices and shake. Strain into a crushed-ice-filled rocks glass. Top up with rosé and garnish with a watermelon wedge, sliced chilli/chile and rosemary sprig. Serve at once with a straw.

Rosemary Syrup

Put 250 ml/1 cup water in a small saucepan with 225 g/1 cup white sugar. Bring to the boil and let simmer until clear and slightly thickened. Take off the heat and add 3 sprigs of fresh rosemary. When cool, strain, discard the rosemary and pour the mixture into a screw-top jar. It will keep in the fridge for up to 3 weeks.

Pinkie Swizzle

This sparkling rum swizzle reinvented is an ice-cold, lip-tingling treat.

40 ml/1½ oz. 100% pomegranate juice
30 ml/1 oz. Bacardi or other white rum
10 ml/¼ oz. sugar syrup
60 ml/2 oz. rosé Prosecco, well-chilled

pomegranate seeds, to garnish
crushed ice
serves 1

Combine the pomegranate juice, rum and syrup in a cocktail shaker with ice cubes and shake until chilled. Strain into a crushed-ice-filled rocks glass and pour in the Prosecco. Garnish with pomegranate seeds and serve at once with a straw.

Rosé, Limoncello & Basil Slush

In Naples, limoncello is often served as a digestif in little freezer-frosted glasses, so it lends itself perfectly to the frosé treatment! This is quite boozy so best served in a small glass.

1 x 750-ml/25-oz. bottle full-flavoured fruity rosé (an Italian Pinot Grigio works well here)

45 ml/1½ oz. limoncello (Italian lemon liqueur)

30 ml/1 oz. Basil Syrup (see page 34)

30 ml/1 oz. freshly squeezed lemon juice

4–6 fresh basil leaves, rinsed and patted dry, plus extra to garnish

lemon zest and freshly ground black pepper (optional), to garnish

serves 4–6

Pour the rosé into a freezerproof container and freeze until solid. Remove from the freezer and allow it to defrost for about 35–40 minutes, until you can break it up with a fork but it's still holding plenty of ice crystals. Scoop into the cup of a blender and add the limoncello, basil syrup, lemon juice and basil leaves. Blend for 30 seconds until foamy and speckled with basil. Pour into serving glasses, then garnish with lemon zest, a basil leaf and black pepper, if using. Serve at once with straws and/or teaspoons.

Rosé, Pink Grapefruit & Rosemary Granita

A tangy alternative to a classic frosé, for those who prefer a less sugary drink.

1 x 750-ml/25-oz. bottle full-flavoured fruity rosé (an Italian Pinot Grigio works well here)

250 ml/1 cup pink grapefruit juice

60 ml/2 oz. Rosemary Syrup (see page 46)

rosemary sprigs and pink grapefruit slices, to garnish

serves 3–4

Pour the rosé into a freezerproof container and freeze until solid. Remove from the freezer and allow it to defrost for about 35–40 minutes, until you can break it up with a fork but it's still holding plenty of ice crystals. Stir in the grapefruit juice and rosemary syrup and return to the freezer for about 30 minutes. Remove from the freezer, break up the crystals with a fork and spoon into glasses. Garnish each serving with a rosemary sprig and grapefruit slice. Serve at once with straws and long spoons.

Punches & Pitchers

Just Peachy Punch

A pale pink Provençal rosé, peach purée and French brandy enjoy a ménage à trois here with delicious results. Oh là là!

4 ripe peaches, stoned/pitted and cut into wedges

75 ml/2½ oz. French brandy

75 ml/2½ oz. peach schnapps

1 x 750-ml/25-oz. bottle well-chilled light, crisp rosé
(a Provençal-style works well here)

375 ml/1½ cups bottled French peach juice or purée (see note)

1–1½ litres/4–6 cups Indian tonic water, well-chilled

peach slices and fresh basil sprigs, to garnish

ice cubes

serves 6—8

Put the peaches in a large jug/pitcher, pour over the brandy and schnapps and leave to marinate for a few hours.

When ready to serve, pour the wine into the jug/pitcher along with the peach juice/nectar and add plenty of ice cubes. Stir and top up to taste with tonic. Pour into ice-cube-filled tumblers, garnish each serving with a peach slice and a sprig of basil and serve at once.

NOTE: If you can't find bottled peach juice or purée, blend about 6 stoned/pitted ripe peaches (to yield 375 ml/1½ cups of juice) and pass the purée through a sieve/strainer to remove any fibre or lumps. Taste and sweeten to taste if necessary with a little sugar syrup before using. It will depend on the ripeness of the peaches used.

Spicy Ginger & Berry Cooler

Here is a super-simple punch that requires the minimum of effort but tastes delicious nonetheless, whilst being lower in alcohol than many punch recipes as it contains no spirits. It needs to sit in the fridge overnight to allow the fruit to macerate in the wine and add flavour. The hint of spice from the ginger ale adds the finishing touch.

100 g/1 cup strawberries, hulled and sliced

100 g/1 cup raspberries

50 g/¼ cup white caster/granulated sugar

1 x 750-ml/25-oz. bottle fruity, sweet rosé (an Italian Montepulciano works well here)

1 litre/4 cups sparkling ginger ale, well chilled

1 orange, thinly sliced, to garnish

ice cubes

serves 6—8

Pour the wine into a large jug/pitcher and add the strawberries, raspberries and sugar. Cover and marinate overnight in the fridge. When ready to serve, pour the ginger ale into the jug/pitcher and stir. Add ice cubes and pour into ice-cube-filled tumblers. Add a few berries to each serving and garnish with orange slices. Serve at once.

The Pink & The Green

A fragrant and delicate drink that is the cocktail equivalent of a fine linen handkerchief spritzed with rosewater. It makes the ideal accompaniment to an elegant afternoon tea and pairs perfectly with cucumber sandwiches and macarons.

1 x 750-ml/25-oz. bottle ripe, fruity rosé (a French Merlot
works well here), well chilled

250 ml/1 cup St-Germain elderflower liqueur (or elderflower cordial
to make a drink that has a lower alcohol content)

125 ml/½ cup freshly squeezed lemon juice

45 ml/1½ oz. Cucumber Syrup (see page 33)

30 ml/1 oz. rosewater

1–1½ litres/4–6 cups Fever-Tree Elderflower Indian
tonic water, well chilled

cucumber slices and lemon wheels

edible rose petals, to garnish

serves 6–8

Pour the rosé, St-Germain elderflower liqueur, lemon juice, cucumber syrup and rosewater into a large punch bowl. Add plenty of ice cubes to chill, then add elderflower tonic to taste. Follow with the cucumber and lemon slices and stir.

Scatter over the rose petals just before serving. Ladle into ice-cube-filled white wine glasses, adding a little of the fruit and edible rose petals to each glass. Serve at once.

Rosé, Bourbon & Blue

I must confess to not being a huge fan of whiskey, but I was blown away by this moreish julep-style punch. The puréed fresh blueberries give the drink both its distinctive flavour and juicy body while the tannin is just detectable underneath the smoky notes of the bourbon. A delicious surprise indeed!

8 tablespoons raw cane sugar

250 g/2 cups fresh blueberries, rinsed and picked over for stems

500 ml/2 cups brewed unsweetened black tea, cooled

330 ml/1⅓ cups dry but fruity rosé (a Chilean Cabernet-blend works well here)

250 ml/1 cup bourbon

175 ml/¾ cup freshly squeezed lemon juice

lemon slices and blueberries, to garnish

ice cubes

serves 6—8

Stir the sugar with 7 tablespoons of hot water in a small bowl until the sugar is dissolved. Transfer to the cup of a blender. Add 65 g/½ cup blueberries to the processor and purée. Set a sieve/strainer over a large jug/pitcher. Strain the blueberry mixture, pressing on the solids with the back of a wooden spoon to extract as much liquid as possible. Discard the solids. Add the cooled tea, rosé, bourbon and lemon juice to the jug/pitcher. Cover and refrigerate until chilled, about 2 hours.

When ready to serve, add the remaining blueberries to the jug/pitcher, fill old-fashioned glasses with ice cubes and divide the drink among the glasses. Garnish each serving with a lemon slice and a blueberry. Serve at once.

Cherry Vanilla Kiss

A cotton-candy inspired treat for those with a passion for all things cherry.

125 ml/½ cup white sugar

400 g/2 cups fresh sweet cherries, stoned/pitted

1 vanilla pod/bean, whole

1 x 750-ml/25-oz. bottle bold, fruity rosé (an Australian Shiraz works well here)

125 ml/½ cup brandy

125 ml/½ cup Morello cherry cordial

65 ml/¼ cup cherry bitters (Peychaud or Angostura can be used if not available)

½ litre/2 cups soda water, chilled

ice cubes

8 vanilla pods/beans, to garnish

serves 8

Bring 125 ml/½ cup water and the sugar to a simmer in a small saucepan, and stir until the sugar has just dissolved. Remove from the heat. Put the cherries and vanilla pod/bean into a large jug/pitcher, pour in the warm syrup and let stand for 5 minutes. Add the wine, brandy, cherry cordial and cherry bitters and stir to combine. Chill for at least 1 hour. When ready to serve, add the soda and pour into ice-cube-filled highball glasses. Garnish each serving with a vanilla pod/bean and serve at once.

Tutti Frutti Summer Sangria

Full of juicy fruit and pink ice cubes, this is as delicious to drink as it is pretty to look at.

2 x 750-ml/25-oz. bottles dark, fruity, very sweet rosé, well chilled (a Californian Zinfandel works well here)

8 sweet cherries, pitted and halved

8 strawberries, hulled and sliced

1–2 white peaches, pitted and sliced

freshly squeezed juice of 1 lime

6 sugar cubes

225 ml/8 oz. vodka

225 ml/1 cup fresh watermelon juice (see page 29)

fresh cherry and lime wedge, to garnish

serves 6

First make the rosé ice cubes. Pour 1 bottle of rosé into ice cube trays and transfer to the freezer. Meanwhile, combine the other ingredients in a large jug/pitcher. Leave for at least 2 hours. When ready to serve, add the rosé ice cubes, add the second bottle of rosé and stir. Pour into glasses, garnish with a cherry and a lime wedge and serve at once.

Sparkling Mediterranean Punch

The scent of thyme will transport you to a village nestled away on a hilltop in Tuscany.
This recipe makes an extra-large quantity so it is ideal for an alfresco party.
You'll need a 3.5-litre/scant 4 quart capacity punch bowl or drinks dispenser to serve.

4 sprigs of fresh thyme, plus extra to garnish

1 x 750-ml/25-oz. bottle Aperol, well chilled

1 x 750-ml/25-oz. bottle dry white vermouth, well chilled (I like to use Lillet)

1 litre/4 cups fresh pink or white grapefruit juice

**1 x 750-ml/25-oz. bottle juicy, sparkling rosé, well chilled (a Cava Rosada
or rosé Prosecco both work well here)**

slices of pink grapefruit, to garnish

ice cubes

serves 20

Combine the thyme sprigs, Aperol, vermouth and grapefruit juice
in a jug/pitcher and chill for at least 2 hours.

Pour into a large punch bowl, add the sparkling rosé and plenty
of ice cubes. Add a few ice cubes and a slice of grapefruit to each
serving glass. Small wine glasses or tumblers can be used.
Pour in the punch and add a sprig of fresh thyme
to each serving to garnish. Serve at once.

Fireside Sangria

Who said rosé was just for summer? Here is a delicious sparkling punch
to cosy up with on colder days. It makes a refreshing and welcome alternative
to the ubiquitous mulled wine at any festive gathering.

about 10 seedless white grapes, halved lengthways

about 10 seedless red grapes, halved lengthways

1 small orange, finely sliced

90 ml/3 oz. Grand Marnier or other orange-flavoured liqueur

90 ml/3 oz. aged sweet red vermouth (I like to use Carpano Antica Formula)

170 ml/¾ cup clementine juice (or blood orange juice also works well)

375 ml/1½ cups fresh, fruity Sauvignon Blanc (preferably from New Zealand)

1 x 750-ml/25-oz. bottle well-chilled sparkling rosé (a pink Champagne
or rosé Prosecco both work well here)

dried orange slices and cinnamon sticks, to garnish

ice cubes

serves 6–8

Put the grapes and orange slices in a punch bowl. Pour in all of the other
ingredients, including plenty of ice cubes and stir.

Serve ladled into ice-filled tumblers or red wine glasses and garnish each
one with a dried orange slice and a cinnamon stick.

Index

28 Day Loan